AMAZING OCEAN LIFE

Sea Stars

by Colleen Sexton

Kaleidoscope
Minneapolis, MN

Where the Quest for Discovery Begins

This edition first published in 2023 by Kaleidoscope Publishing, Inc.

Kaleidoscope Publishing, Inc.
6012 Blue Circle Drive
Minnetonka, MN 55343

Library of Congress Control Number
2022937342

ISBN
978-1-64519-564-1 (library bound)
978-1-64519-634-1 (ebook)

Precious McKenzie, Developmental Editor

Table of Contents

Sea Stars Everywhere

Ocean waves wash over sea stars. The sea stars are many shapes, sizes, and colors. Some are orange, some are blue, and some are yellow.

FUN FACT
There are about 2,000 different kinds of sea stars.

Where Do Sea Stars Live?

Sea stars

Arctic Ocean
North America
Atlantic Ocean
Europe
Asia
Africa
South America
Pacific Ocean
Indian Ocean
Australia
Antarctica

Sea stars are found in oceans all over the world.

They live in **shallow** water near shore and in deep water on the sea floor.

Star Bodies

FUN FACT
Sea stars do not have a brain or blood.

Sea stars have bumpy bodies covered with **spines**.

Their arms are called **rays**. All sea stars have at least five rays. Some have more than 40!

Parts of a Sea Star

If a sea star loses a ray, a new ray grows back!

The tip of each ray has an eye. A sea star uses its eyes to tell light from dark.

On the Move

Sea stars travel. A sea star moves on hundreds of little **tube feet**.

The tube feet end in **suckers** that stick to hard places.

The sea star creeps across sand and crawls up seaweed. It climbs over rocks and **coral reefs**.

Sometimes big groups of sea stars travel together. They go to deeper water to feed.

FUN FACT
A group of sea stars is called a galaxy.

Good Hunting

Sea stars hunt. A sea star smells a clam and sets off to catch its **prey**.

The sea star moves slowly to sneak up on the clam and grab it.

What Do Sea Stars Eat?

The sea star uses its tube feet to pull apart the clam's **shell**.

The sea star pushes its stomach out from the middle of its body.

Sometimes sea stars are prey. Birds, sea turtles, and otters eat sea stars.

stomach

The sea star feeds on the clam.
It leaves the empty shell behind.

FUN FACT

Sea stars can go months without food.

The sea star pulls its stomach back in and crawls away to hunt again.

Photo Glossary

coral reef: A form of rock made of old and new corals. Sea stars climb over coral reefs.

prey: An animal that is hunted by another animal for food. A sea star can smell prey like a clam.

rays: Arms that grow out from the center of a sea star. Rays can be short and wide or long and narrow.

shallow: When water is not deep. Some sea stars live in shallow water near the shore.

shell: A hard outer covering. Many animals that sea stars eat have shells.

spines: Hard, sharp growths that stick out from an animal's body to protect it. Sea stars have bumpy bodies covered with spines.

suckers: Round cup-shaped parts on the end of a sea star's tube feet. Suckers can bend and stretch to hold on to things.

tube feet: Small tube-shaped feet on the bottom of sea star's rays used to move around. A sea star moves on hundreds of little tube feet.

Read More

Zimmerman, Adeline J. *Sea Stars.* World of Ocean Animals. Minneapolis, MN: Jump!, 2022.

Zobel, Derek. *Sea Stars.* Ocean Animals. Minneapolis, MN: Bellwether Media, 2021.

Zommer, Yuval. *The Big Book of the Blue*. New York, NY: Thames & Hudson, 2018.

Websites

Factsurfer.com gives you a safe, fun way to find more information.

1. Go to www.factsurfer.com.
2. Enter "Sea Stars" into the search box and click
3. Select your book cover to see a list of related websites.

About the Author

Colleen Sexton is a writer and editor. She is the author of more than one hundred nonfiction books for kids on topics ranging from astronauts to glaciers to elephants. She lives in Minnesota.

INDEX

PHOTO CREDITS

The images in this book are reproduced through Shutterstock: Kim Reinick 1; Maryna Kulchytska 3; Paper Street Design 4; nito 5; Wassana Panapute 6; Rich Carey 7; meunierd 8; Rattiya Thongdumhyu 9, 17, 22; JaysonPhotography 9; Katherine Wallis 9, 11; valda butterworth 9, 22; Fotopogledi 10; RealityImages 10; Benny Marty 12; Dan Bagur 13; Kriwoot Boontan 14; Michelle Gilbert 14; Davdeka 14; Damsea 15, 17, 23; Joe Belanger 16; Spayder pauk_79 17; Aleksandar Dickov 17; Lotus Images 17; Potapov Alexander 17; Jiang Zhongyan 17, 22; Mark Conlin 18; scubaluna 18; Michaelerch 19, 22; Vojce 21; Just dance 21; Soonios Pro 22; Joanna Szypulska 22; Belight 22; Irina Markova 22. Cover: Kim Reinick, Solarisys. Reproduced through Alamy Stock Photo: Mark Conlin 18; Andrey Nekrasov 20.